EXPLORING THE UNIVERSE

The SUN and MOON

ROBIN KERROD

RAINTREE
STECK-VAUGHN
PUBLISHERS

A Harcourt Company

Austin   New York
www.raintreesteckvaughn.com

**First American edition published in 2002
by Raintree Steck-Vaughn Publishers**

© 2002 by Graham Beehag Books

Raintree Steck-Vaughn Publishers
4515 Seton Center Parkway
Austin, Texas 78755

Website address: www.raintreesteckvaughn.com

Library of Congress Cataloging-in-Publication Data

Kerrod, Robin.
    Exploring the sun and moon / Robin Kerrod.
        p. cm. — (Exploring the universe)
    Includes bibliographical references and index.
    Summary: Discusses the differences and similarities between the sun
    and the moon.
    ISBN 0-7398-2818-5
    1. Sun—Juvenile literature. 2. Moon—Juvenile literature [1. Sun.
    2. Moon.] I. Title

    QB521.5 .K45 2001
    523—dc21   2001031675

Printed and bound in the United States.

1 2 3 4 5 6 7 8 9 0 05 04 03 02 01

Contents

Introduction

The Sun and the Moon are the two heavenly bodies that dominate our skies—the Sun by day and the Moon by night. When the Moon is full, they both appear about the same size in the sky. This does not mean that they are really the same size, of course. In reality, the Sun is 400 times wider across (in diameter) than the Moon. It looks to us to be the same size as the Moon only because it is 400 times farther away.

The Sun and the Moon are two very different kinds of bodies. The Sun is a great ball of searing hot gases that pours out enormous amounts of light and heat into space. The Moon is a drab ball of cold rock that shines only because it reflects the Sun's light.

And there are still more differences. The Moon circles around Earth, once a month. Earth circles around the Sun once a year. Earth circles around, or orbits, the Sun along with eight other bodies, the planets. Earth itself is a planet. The planets are the main members of the solar system. (Solar means having to do with the Sun.)

In our corner of space, the Moon is not particularly important at all. There are many other moons. The Moon is not essential to life on Earth. But there is only one Sun. Without its light and heat, Earth would be a dark, cold, and dead world, without life as we know it.

In part because it is so much closer to Earth, we know more about the Moon than we do about the Sun. Astronomers have been studying the Moon for hundreds of years, with their eyes and through telescopes. More recently, space probes have explored it, and astronauts have roamed across its surface and brought back samples of rocks and soil. It is likely that one day soon humans will return to the Moon and set up permanent bases there.

The Moon as Apollo astronauts saw it. The bright areas are older highland regions, thickly covered with craters. The dark areas are younger flat plains, which early astronomers thought might be seas.

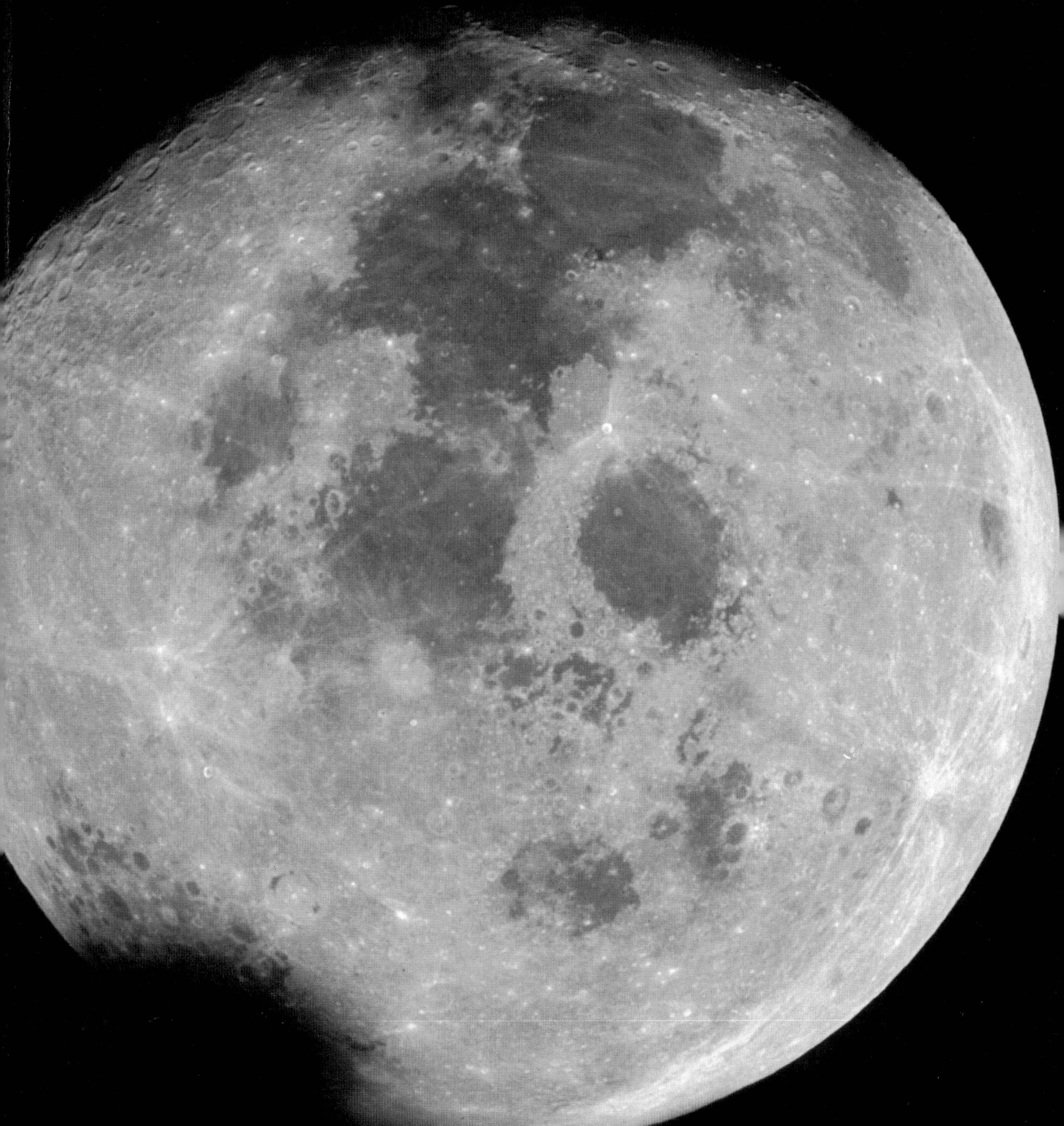

OUR STAR, THE SUN

The Sun is Earth's local star. It looks much bigger than the other stars we see in the heavens only because it is much closer. The Sun is very special to us, but it is not special in the universe. Indeed, it is a very ordinary star—there are billions like it.

The Sun is about 93 million miles (150 million km) away from Earth. This may seem a great distance, but in space it is just a short step. The next nearest star, called Proxima Centauri, lies more than 25 trillion miles (40 trillion km) away. The light from this star takes more than 4 years to reach Earth. Sunlight takes only about 8½ minutes to reach Earth.

Compared with Earth, the Sun is enormous. It could swallow more than a million bodies the size of Earth. It measures about 865,000 miles (1,400,000 km) in diameter.

Among stars, the Sun is much bigger than some but much smaller than others. Huge stars called supergiants are hundreds of times bigger in diameter, which is why astronomers classify the Sun as a dwarf star. They call it a yellow dwarf because it gives off yellowish light.

To people on Earth, it appears that the Sun moves across the sky every day. But it is not the Sun that is moving but Earth. Earth spins around in space on its axis, which makes it seem that the Sun is moving through the sky.

But the Sun does move in two ways. One, it spins around on its axis—or revolves—just like Earth does. The Sun, however takes about 25 days to revolve once. Two, the Sun is traveling through space at a fantastic speed—about 12 miles (20 km) per second. The billions of other stars in our local star system, or galaxy, are traveling at similar speeds.

Like other stars, the Sun was born in a nebula, a great cloud of gas and dust that once existed in our corner of space. Astronomers estimate that this happened about 4.6 billion years ago. The cloud shrunk into a ball, which became hotter and hotter until it began to shine as a star. The rest of the Sun's family of planets and other bodies formed at the same time.

The fiery ball of the Sun, pictured by the *SOHO* probe. Bright flares are erupting in several places, while a huge looping fountain of flaming gas is shooting thousands of miles above the surface (top right).

photosphere

convection zone

radiation zone

core

chromosphere

Inside the Sun

Like the other stars, the Sun is a great ball of gas. Actually it is a mixture of many gases. Astronomers learn which gases are present in the Sun by examining the light it gives out. They have learned that the most common gas is hydrogen, which is the lightest gas of all. The next most common gas is helium.

Along with hydrogen and helium, astronomers know that the Sun contains many other substances, such as iron, calcium, and sodium. These substances are solids on Earth but are gases on the Sun because it is so hot.

Hot Stuff

What is the source of the heat and light given off by the Sun? It cannot be produced by burning an ordinary fuel such as natural gas, or methane. If the Sun burned such a fuel, it would have burned itself out billions of years ago. The Sun produces its energy by nuclear reactions. These are reactions in which atoms of elements take part. Atoms are among the tiniest particles of substances that can be measured. The center of an atom is called the nucleus, which is where the term "nuclear" comes from.

Fusing Atoms

In the main nuclear reaction that takes place in the Sun, atoms of hydrogen are made to fuse, or join, together. When this happens, fantastic amounts of energy are given off in the form of light and heat. This kind of reaction takes place in the center, or core, of the Sun, where temperatures reach 15,000,000°C or more.

From the core, the energy travels outward towards the Sun's surface. It may take as long as 100,000 years to reach the surface. First it travels as radiation (waves), then on moving gas currents—rather like the hot air currents you can feel when you put your hand over a radiator at home.

When the energy does reach the surface, it escapes into space as light, heat, and other radiation. The Sun's surface is called the photosphere, meaning the light-sphere. It is very much cooler than the core, with a temperature of about 5,500°C.

Carry on Shining

The nuclear reactions that occur in the Sun use up huge amounts of hydrogen—some 600 million tons every second. But the Sun is so big that it has enough hydrogen to last for about another 5 billion years.

When all the hydrogen is used up, the Sun will start to die. First, it will swell up to become a kind of star called a red giant. Then it will shrink until it becomes a white dwarf—a tiny, very dense body only about the size of Earth.

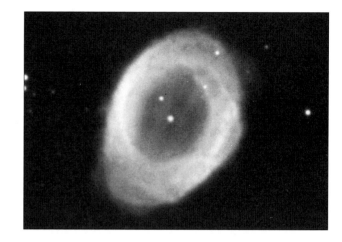

When the Sun dies, it will first expand into a red giant before shrinking again. Then it will throw off masses of gas to form a planetary nebula rather like the Ring Nebula (above). Over time, all that will be left is a tiny hot ball of matter—a white dwarf.

Sun

Red giant

planetary nebula

white dwarf

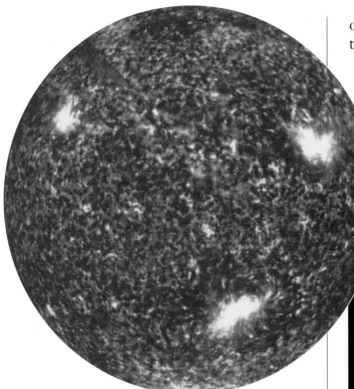

Above: The Sun's surface has a speckled, or grainy, appearance, which astronomers call granulation. The three bright patches in the picture are violent explosions called flares.

The Solar Atmosphere

The photosphere forms the outer layer of the Sun. It is about 200 miles (320 km) thick. But the Sun does not end at the photosphere's outer layer because it has an atmosphere, or layer of gases, around it, just as the Earth does.

The lower part of the Sun's atmosphere is called the chromosphere, or color sphere. This is because it has a pinkish color. A thinner outer atmosphere begins about 3,000 miles (5,000 km) above the surface. It is known as the corona, which means "crown." It extends into space for millions of miles.

Because the photosphere is so blindingly bright, we usually cannot see the chromosphere or corona. We can see them only during a total eclipse of the Sun when the Moon blots out the Sun's glare.

During an eclipse, the chromosphere can be seen as a pink ring around the dark Moon. The corona is much more spectacular, billowing out from the Sun and stretching pearly white into space for a vast distance.

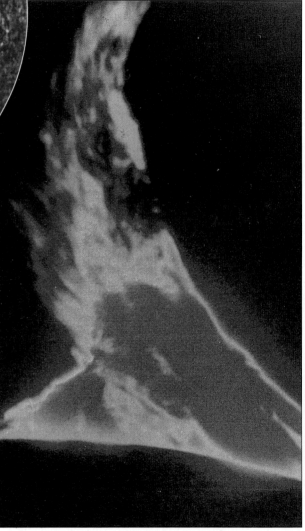

Above: A huge tongue of flame leaps above the Sun's surface. It is a fountain of hot gas known as a prominence. In a matter of hours, prominences can climb 100,000 miles into space.

The Stormy Surface

The photosphere looks glaringly bright all over. But closer inspection—by special instruments—shows that its surface is actually a patchwork of tiny bright and dark areas. They look rather like grains of wheat, and astronomers call them granules. Each granule is a little rising column of gas that carries heat from below to the surface.

Larger bright and dark regions constantly appear and disappear on the photosphere. The most obvious are dark ones that look rather like ink blots. They are known as sunspots. Sunspots are regions that are about 1,500°C cooler than their surroundings. Sunspots come and go in a predictable way over a period of 11 years. This period is known as the sunspot cycle.

Fountains and Flares

Sunspots are caused by changes in the Sun's magnetism. They trigger off other spectacular happenings, such as prominences. These great fountain-like streams of glowing gas may leap above the Sun for hundreds of thousand of miles. They often form into loops, following invisible lines of magnetism.

Sometimes, around new sunspots, there are enormous explosions called flares. For a few minutes, a flare can become the brightest thing on the Sun. It gives off not only light but also invisible radiation, such as X-rays and radio waves. Flares also give off atomic particles that flow out into space.

Above: This picture highlights regions of intense magnetism on the Sun's surface. They are found around sunspots.

Left: A typical sunspot group, showing darker (umbra) and lighter (penumbra) regions. Sunspot groups can spread over tens of thousands of miles.

All these rays or waves have something in common. They are tiny electrical and magnetic vibrations known as electromagnetic waves. They differ in their wavelength—the distance between the same point in two successive waves.

The Short and the Long

Gamma rays, X-rays, and UV rays have shorter wavelengths than light rays. All can be harmful to humans. Earth's atmosphere blocks all the Sun's gamma and X-rays and most of its UV rays. The UV rays that get through are the ones that darken or even burn our skin when we go out in the Sun.

Heat rays (also called infrared rays), microwaves, and radio waves have longer wavelengths than light. They are not as harmful as the shorter rays. Earth's atmosphere blocks some heat rays and microwaves, but it lets through radio waves.

The Solar Wind

The Sun not only gives off radiation, as light and heat, but also streams of atomic particles. The particles flow into space, creating what is called the solar wind.

The Sun's Rays

The Sun gives off most of the energy it produces as visible light and heat. It also gives off energy as other invisible rays. These include gamma rays, X-rays, ultraviolet (UV) rays, microwaves, and radio waves.

Below: An illustration of the electromagnetic spectrum, running from gamma rays to radio waves. Gamma rays have the shortest wavelengths, starting at about one 30-billionth of an inch, or one trillionth of a meter. Radio waves have the longest wavelengths—up to hundreds of miles.

short waves

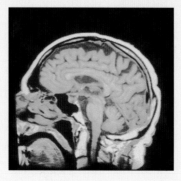

gamma rays

X rays

ultraviolet rays

The solar wind flows out past and beyond the planets. Usually, it takes about four or five days to reach Earth. Earth's magnetism forms a kind of invisible shield that helps protect us from the wind and its particles, which could be harmful to us.

Near the North and South Poles, however, some of these particles reach the atmosphere. There, they collide with air molecules, transmit extra energy, and make them glow.

Lights in the Sky

From the ground, the glow appears as shimmering curtains of colored light known as the aurora. In the Northern Hemisphere, it is called the aurora borealis, or Northern Lights. In the Southern Hemisphere, it is called the aurora australis, or Southern Lights.

Usually the solar wind blows steadily, rather like a gentle breeze on Earth. But when there is great sunspot activity and solar flares erupt, the Sun gives off many more particles. Then the solar wind blows strongly, like a gale on Earth. This produces brilliant auroras in the atmosphere and upsets Earth's magnetism—causing what are called magnetic storms. These storms can disturb electricity sources and radio communications.

Above: A display of the aurora borealis, or Northern Lights. Broad, colorful streamers light up the sky, constantly changing and rippling like a moving curtain.

long waves

visible light

infrared rays

microwaves

radio waves

The Sun's Family

Earth is one of nine planets that circle in space around the Sun. These planets are the main bodies in the solar system. They are scattered at great distances from one another. Most of the solar system just consists of empty space.

The Earth and its three neighbors in space—Mercury, Venus, and Mars—are quite close together in the inner part of the solar system. The planets in the outer solar system—Jupiter, Saturn, Uranus, Neptune, and Pluto—are much farther apart.

The diagram shows the orbits of the planets drawn to scale. Notice that the orbits of all the planets except Pluto are in much the same plane. This means that they would lie on or close to an imaginary flat sheet in space. But Pluto travels quite far above and below it.

Size Matters

The diagram also shows the great difference in sizes among the planets. The four inner planets are tiny in comparison with the next four huge outer planets. They are also quite different in composition, or what they are made of.

The four inner planets are made up mainly of rock, while the four large outer planets are made up mainly of gas and liquid gas. The farthest planet, tiny Pluto, is different again, being made up of rock and ice.

Other Bits and Pieces

Besides the planets, there are many other smaller bodies in the solar system. Most planets have one or more satellites, or bodies, circling them. Earth has only one—the Moon—but Saturn and Uranus each have at least 18.

Another major group of bodies are the asteroids. They are found in a wide band, or belt, roughly midway between the orbits of Mars and Jupiter. Even the biggest asteroid, Ceres, is only about 600 miles (950 km) in diameter. Most of the thousands of asteroids discovered by astronomers are much smaller.

The comets that occasionally appear in our skies are small icy bodies that journey

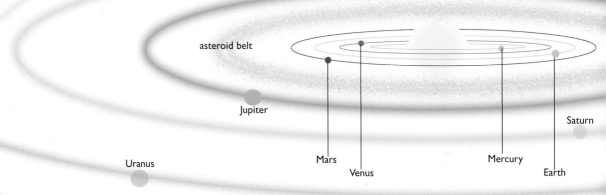

in towards the Sun from the most distant regions of the solar system.

The space between the planets also contains even smaller bits of rock and metal. These bits rain down on Earth all the time, burning up as they hit the upper air. We see them as fiery streaks called meteors, which are also popularly known as falling or shooting stars.

Pulling Power

All these bodies in the solar system—planets, moons, asteroids, comets, and little chunks of matter—are all held together by the Sun's gravity. The Sun has some 750 times more mass that all the other bodies in the solar system put together. This gives it an enormously powerful gravitational force—so powerful that it can attract icy comets only a few miles in width that are located trillions of miles away.

Below: The orbits of the nine planets around the Sun, drawn roughly to scale. They occupy a region of space some 7 billion miles (12 billion km) across.

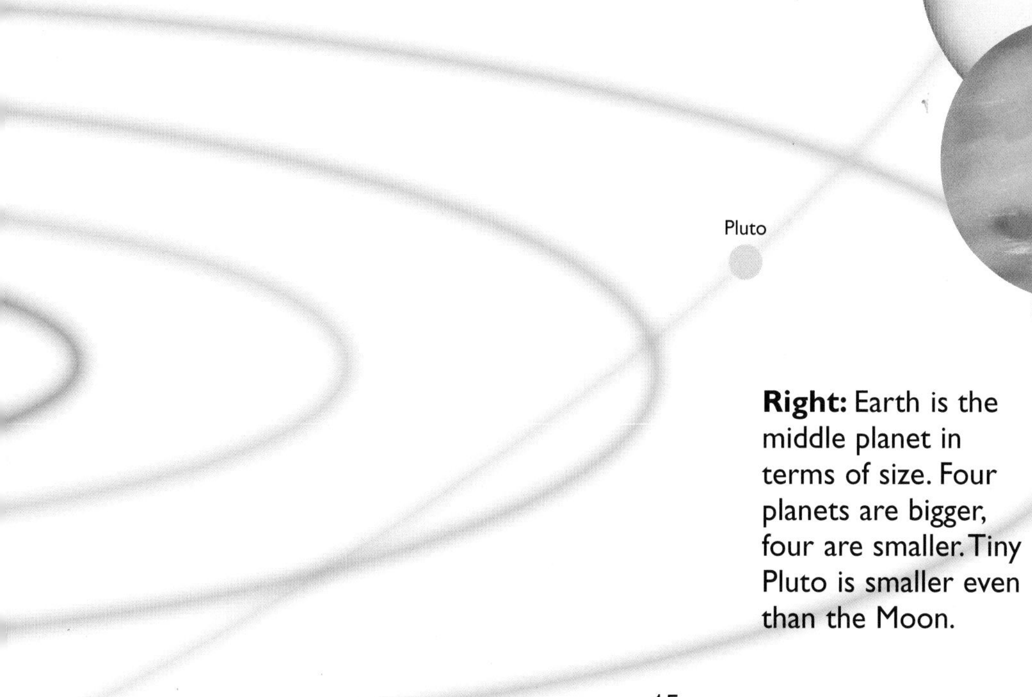

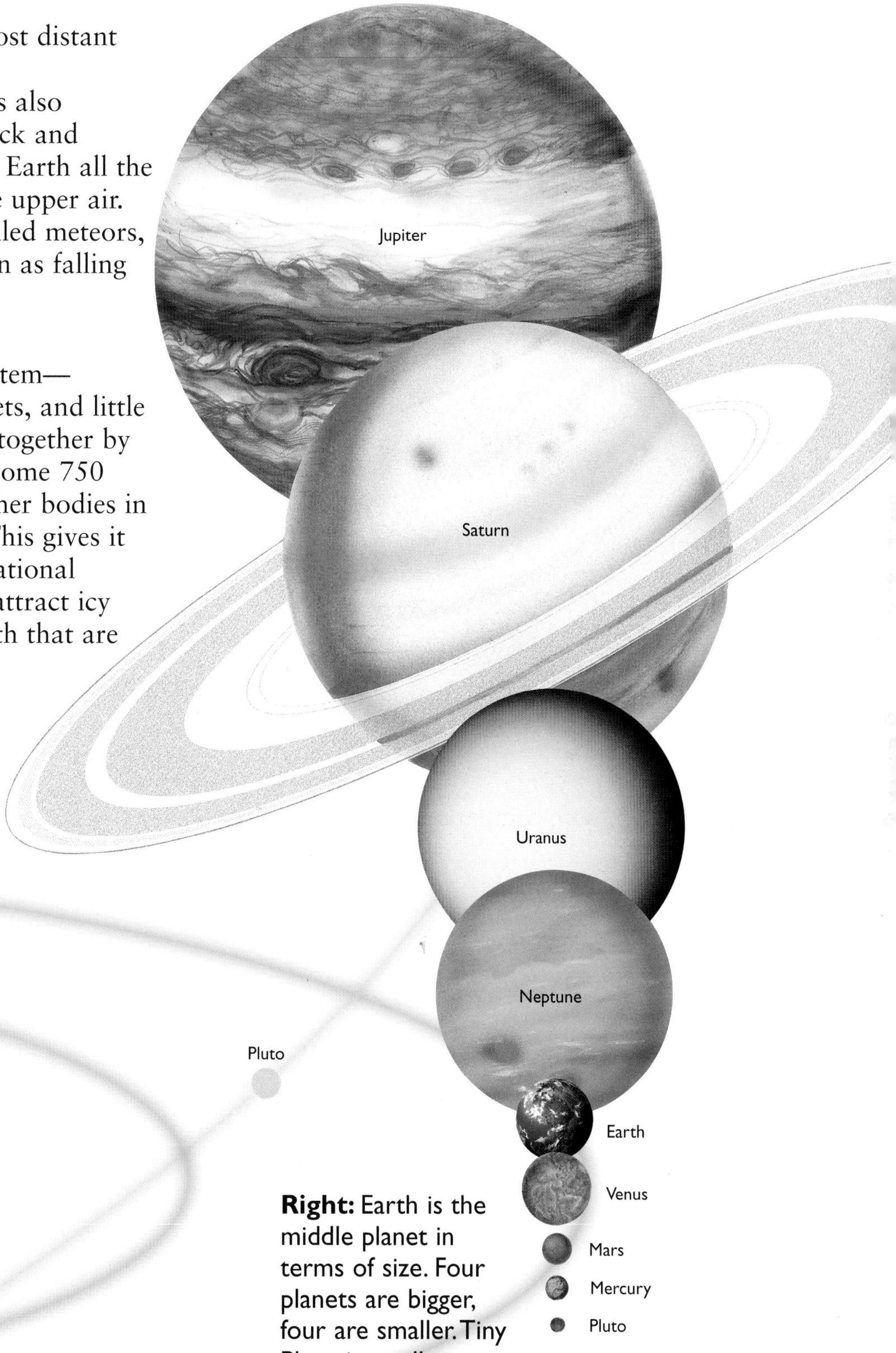

Jupiter

Saturn

Uranus

Neptune

Pluto

Earth

Venus

Right: Earth is the middle planet in terms of size. Four planets are bigger, four are smaller. Tiny Pluto is smaller even than the Moon.

Mars

Mercury

Pluto

SUN AND EARTH

Life on Earth could not exist without the Sun. Its light and heat brighten and warm our world and make it a suitable home for human beings and millions of other living things. It helps determine the weather and creates our climate. It helps us measure time.

Even prehistoric peoples realized how important the Sun was. Many early civilizations worshipped the Sun as a god. More than 4,000 years ago, the ancient Egyptians worshipped the Sun god Ra and pictured him sailing across the heavens during the day. More recently, in Central and South America, the Inca, Aztec, and Mayan peoples centered their religion on Sun worship. They practiced human sacrifice on a vast scale to insure that the Sun rose every day.

Until only about 550 years ago, most people thought that the Sun traveled around the Earth. It certainly appears to every day. In the 15th century, a Polish churchman and astronomer named Nicolaus Copernicus suggested that Earth orbited the Sun. This marked the beginning of the concept of the Sun-centered, or solar, system. Science has since proven that Copernicus was right.

Earth is located in just the right place in the solar system for the creation and sustenance of life. It receives just the right amount of heat from the Sun to keep it at a comfortable temperature for plant and animal life.

If Earth were closer to the Sun, it would be too hot for liquid water—for life. Look at the planet Venus, which is closer to the Sun—it is hotter than an oven. On the other hand, if Earth were much farther away from the Sun, it would be too cold for liquid water—and for life as we know it. For example, Mars, which is farther away from the Sun, has no life on it.

Earth teems with life in great variety. The tiger is one of the several million different species (kinds) of animals and plants found on Earth.

"Spaceship Earth,"
photographed by Apollo
astronauts. The overall color
of Earth is blue because this
is the color of the great
oceans that cover more than
two-thirds of the surface.

Left: The ancient Egyptians thought that the god Ra carried the Sun across the heavens every day in a boat.

Sun Time

To people on Earth, the Sun seems to travel across the sky every day. It rises above the horizon in the east in the early morning, then travels westward, seeming to climb all the while. It reaches its highest point in the sky at noon, or midday. In the afternoon, still traveling westward, it gradually sinks lower in the sky. In the evening, it sets beneath the horizon in the west.

The time between when the Sun reaches its highest point in the sky one day and the time it reaches its highest point the next day is always the same. This is the period of time we call a day. The day is one of our basic units for measuring time. We split this natural division of time artificially into 24 hours, each hour into 60 minutes, and each minute into 60 seconds.

In a Spin

As Copernicus pointed out centuries ago, the Sun does not actually travel around Earth. It only seems to, and that is because Earth itself spins around once every day. Earth spins around on its axis in space from west to east, and this makes the Sun appear to

Left: The astronomical clock at Hampton Court, in London, England. It shows not only the time of day but such things as the phases of the Moon, the time of the year, and the constellation of the zodiac.

Opposite: Earth spins around on its axis once a day, and it takes 365¼ days, or 1 year, to travel once in its orbit around the Sun. The day and the year are the two basic units by which we measure time.

travel in the opposite direction—from east to west.

The Solar Year

Earth travels around the Sun in a nearly circular path. It spins around 365 and one-quarter times while it travels one complete circle, or orbit. In other words, it takes Earth 365¼ days to orbit the Sun once. This is another basic unit of time, which we call the year.

We use the day and the year to make up our calendar—a standard way of dividing up time. As well as the day and the year, our calendar also uses months, a time period loosely based on the time it takes the Moon to complete its phases (see pages 26–27).

Our calendar year is 365 days, except for every fourth year, when an extra day is added at the end of February, the shortest month in the calendar year. This extra day is added to account for the difference of one-quarter day between the calendar year and the natural, or solar year.

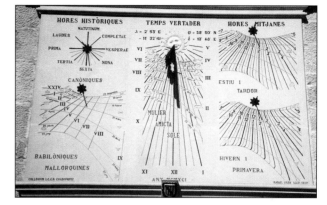

An unusual, modern Spanish sundial, designed to be accurate during different seasons of the year.

Leap years are usually years that can be divided by four, or by 400 for beginning-of-the century years, such as 2000. Even so this system does not keep our calendar year exactly in time with the solar year. So sometimes extra seconds—leap seconds—are added to keep our calendar in step with the workings of the heavens.

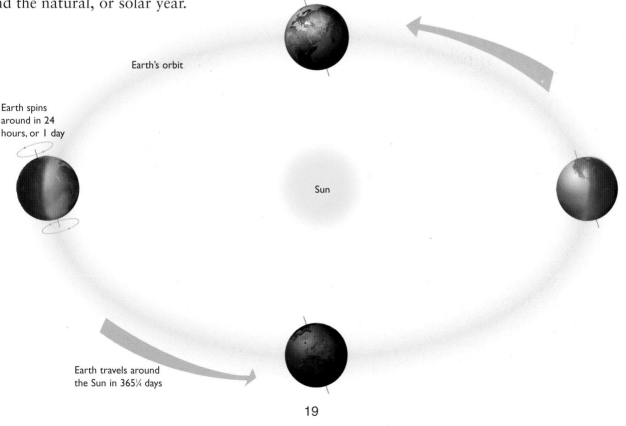

Earth's orbit

Earth spins around in 24 hours, or 1 day

Sun

Earth travels around the Sun in 365¼ days

The Weather Machine

The Sun pours out enormous amounts of energy into space. And only a tiny fraction of it—one two-billionth—reaches Earth. But even this tiny amount is enough to warm the Earth and make its weather.

Beams of sunlight

equator

The warmth, or temperature, of our surroundings is the most important feature of Earth's weather. It affects all the other features, too, such as the movement of air and the amount of moisture in the air.

For example, air rises over hot regions, creating areas of low pressure. It sinks over cold ones, creating areas of high pressure. Air masses flow from high to low pressure, creating winds and even larger movements of the air.

The Sun heats the water in oceans and lakes, and makes it evaporate, or escape into the air as vapor (gas). The water vapor rises into the air and cools down. When it cools sufficiently, it turns back into droplets of water, which collect to form clouds. When the drops get big enough, they fall back to the ground as rain or even snow if the temperature is low enough.

Snow and the Sun

Of course, not all places on Earth have the same weather. For example, in winter, many people from snowy New England go on vacation to Florida, where it is sunnier and much warmer. In general, throughout the

Left: A beam of sunlight covers the smallest area at the Equator. Its energy is most concentrated here, so this region is warmest. Away from the Equator, beams spread out over wider areas because of Earth's curve. Their energy is more dispersed, and so these areas are cooler.

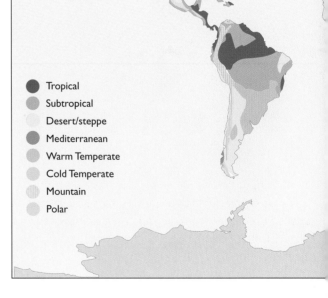

- Tropical
- Subtropical
- Desert/steppe
- Mediterranean
- Warm Temperate
- Cold Temperate
- Mountain
- Polar

year Florida has warmer weather than New England—it has a warmer climate.

Florida has a warmer climate than New England because it is nearer to Earth's Equator. Places near the Equator enjoy the warmest climate on Earth because throughout the entire year they receive the most direct sunlight.

Because the Earth is round, places farther away from the Equator receive less direct sunlight. To people living there, the Sun never appears to climb as high in the sky as it does to people at the Equator. Accordingly, those places get less direct sunlight. The farther a place is away from the Equator, the lower the Sun will climb and the cooler it will be.

Places near the North and South Poles are coldest of all.

Although the climate of a place depends mainly on its distance from the Equator, it can also be affected by other things. For example, places on sea coasts enjoy a warmer climate than places in the middle of the continents. This is because water retains heat better than land does. Ocean currents affect climate, too. For example, parts of northwestern Europe enjoy a mild climate because the Gulf Stream helps warm them.

World Climates

Scientists divide the world into a number of regions that have the same kind of climate. They enjoy similar temperatures and have similar rainfall throughout the year. The map shows the world divided into eight kinds of climate, or climatic, zones. Each zone has its own kind of vegetation and wildlife, which can thrive in that particular climate.

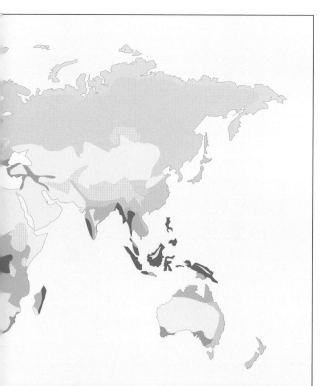

Climates around the world. Hot, dry deserts cover huge expanses of Earth's surface. Warm temperate regions are productive regions for agriculture. Vast conifer forests thrive in the northern cool temperate regions.

New England regularly has snow in winter, while Florida enjoys the sunshine and a warmer climate.

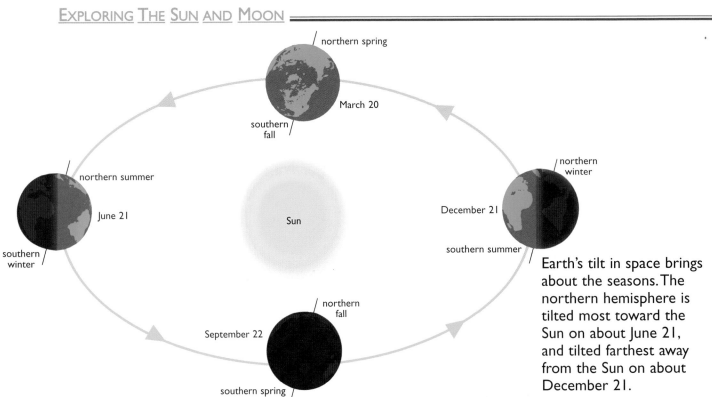

northern spring

March 20

southern fall

northern summer

June 21

southern winter

Sun

northern winter

December 21

southern summer

northern fall

September 22

southern spring

Earth's tilt in space brings about the seasons. The northern hemisphere is tilted most toward the Sun on about June 21, and tilted farthest away from the Sun on about December 21.

Season by Season

Generally, the weather experienced in a particular place depends not just on its location on Earth but on the time of year. For example, much of the United States, and the rest of the northern hemisphere, is cold in December and days are short. By March the weather is warming up and the days are getting longer. June sees hot weather and long days. By September, temperatures are cooler and the days get shorter again. The same pattern is repeated every year. It is a natural rhythm of nature. In the southern hemisphere, the seasons are the direct opposite of what they are in the north. When it is winter in the northern hemisphere, it is summer in the southern hemisphere, and so on.

The regular changes in temperature and the lengths of the day and night divide the year into periods we call the seasons. Over much of the world there are four seasons—winter, spring, summer, and fall (or autumn).

In some parts of the world, there are not four distinct seasons. Near the Equator, the weather hardly changes at all as the months go by. On either side of the Equator, in the tropics, there are only two seasons, a dry one and a rainy one.

Earth's Tilt
What causes the changing seasons? It is the

way Earth moves in space in relation to the Sun. As Earth travels in its yearlong orbit around the Sun, it spins around like a top on its axis, which is an imaginary line through its center and the North and South Poles.

But Earth does not spin upright as it circles the Sun. Its axis is tilted (at an angle of 23½ degrees). It remains tilted at this angle all the time and always points in the same direction in space.

This means that as Earth travels in its orbit, the axis points first towards, then away from, the Sun. So different places on Earth are tilted more towards the Sun at some times than they are other times. The more they are tilted towards the Sun, the warmer they will be. The more they are tilted away from the Sun, the cooler they will be. This is what brings about the change of temperature with the seasons.

Changing Skies

You can follow the changing seasons during the day by watching how high the Sun climbs in the sky at midday. It climbs highest in summer and lowest in winter. We can also follow the seasons by watching the night sky.

Earth circles around the Sun during the year. On any particular date, we look out at night in a particular direction in space. We see certain star groups, or constellations. As the days and months go by and Earth moves in its orbit, we look into a slightly different spot in space, so we see different constellations.

For example, in North America, the constellation Orion appears in the southern part of the evening sky in the winter. But in the fall, the constellation Pegasus appears in that part of the sky.

Left: "Down under" in Australia in December, the people are enjoying summer. They often celebrate Christmas by having parties on the beach.

Right: In the tropical rain forests that grow near the Equator, the climate stays the same all year: it is always hot and wet.

THE SILVERY MOON

The Moon is Earth's closest neighbor in space and its constant companion. As circles around Earth once a month, it appears to change shape, from a slim crescent to a full circle, then back again. The pull of the Moon's gravity causes t daily rise and fall of the oceans that we call the tides.

The Moon is Earth's only natural satellite. It is quite a small body, with a diameter of 2,160 miles (3,476 km). This is about one-quarter the diameter of Earth, and nearly three-quarters the distance across the United States.

Although the Moon is relatively small, it dominates the night sky because it is so close to Earth. On average, it is only about 239,000 miles (384,000 km) away. The next nearest body to us in space—Venus—is more than 100 times farther away. It never comes closer to Earth than 26,000,000 miles (42,000,000 km).

Other planets besides Earth also have moons, of course. Among them, Earth's moon ranks fifth in size. Bigger than the Moon are the three largest of Jupiter's moons—Ganymede, Callisto, and Io—and Saturn's moon Titan. However, Earth's moon is much bigger in relation to the size of its parent planet than are these other moons. Astronomers sometimes refer to Earth and the Moon together as a double planet.

Long ago, people worshipped the Moon. Just as the Sun brought light to the world by day, so the silvery Moon brought light by night. The ancient Romans called their Moon goddess Diana. In Latin, the language spoken by the ancient Romans, the word for Moon was "luna," and from this we get our word "lunar," meaning to do with the Moon.

Some ancient peoples also believed that the Moon somehow affected people's minds, particularly the full moon. They believed that exposure to moonlight could cause a person to go mad. This led to the term "lunatic" being used for an insane person.

The full moon as seen from Earth

This astronaut's view of a full moon looks different
from the full moon we see from Earth. The right-hand
side of the photograph reveals part of the far side of
the Moon, which we can never see from Earth.

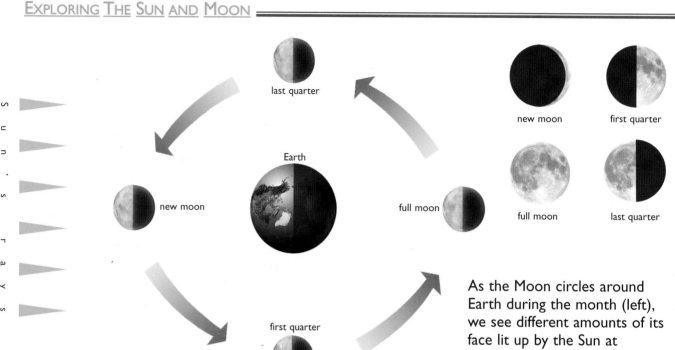

Sun's rays

last quarter

Earth

new moon

full moon

first quarter

new moon

first quarter

full moon

last quarter

As the Moon circles around Earth during the month (left), we see different amounts of its face lit up by the Sun at different times (right). These views are the main phases.

Moon Motions

The Moon gives off no light of its own. The Moon appears to shine because it reflects light given off by the Sun. The Moon does not reflect sunlight very well—it reflects less than ten percent of the light that falls on it. Astronomers say it has a low albedo ("whiteness").

As the moon circles the Earth, we see different amounts of it lit up at different times each month. This accounts for what we refer to as the "phases" of the moon.

Monthly Motion

The Moon circles once around Earth every 27⅓ days. During this time, Earth completes part of its yearlong orbit around the Sun. It takes 29½ days for the Moon to complete its phases—to go through all the stages of illumination in which it appears in the sky.

This lunar period is one of the great natural divisions of time. Early peoples used this lunar month as the basis of their calendars. Today, we base our calendar on the solar year and use months of different numbers of days so that they fit into this year.

Waxing and Waning

The actual shape, or phase, of the Moon we can see at any time depends on where the Moon, the Sun, and Earth are located in space. Once a month, the Moon moves roughly in line between the Sun and Earth in space. Then we can't see it in the night sky because the Sun lights up only its hidden far side. The nearside that faces us remains dark, in shadow. We call this phase of the Moon the new moon.

A day or so after new moon, the Sun lights up the edge of the nearside, and we see the Moon as a crescent, or bow shape. A week later, the Moon, the Sun, and Earth are again roughly lined up in space. The Moon is now on the opposite side of Earth from the Sun. And so the Sun lights up all the nearside of the Moon in the night sky.

Left: The full moon phase, which we see once a month. One of its most prominent features is the bright ray system around the crater Tycho (lower center).

Below: The thin sliver of the crescent moon, when the Moon is 27 days old. Soon the Moon will disappear completely, at the next new moon.

A werewolf is on the prowl! The idea of the werewolf, a man who turns into a wolf at the time of the full moon, is a favorite theme in horror movies.

We call this phase the first quarter. A week later the Sun lights up all the nearside, and we call this phase the full moon. During the time the Moon has been growing from a crescent to full, we say that is has been waxing. After full moon, the amount of the nearside lit up by the Sun gets smaller as time goes by. A week after full moon, only half is lit up. We call this phase the last quarter. And a week later only a thin crescent can be seen. Then the Moon disappears completely—it is the next new moon. During the time the Moon has been shrinking in size, we say it has been waning.

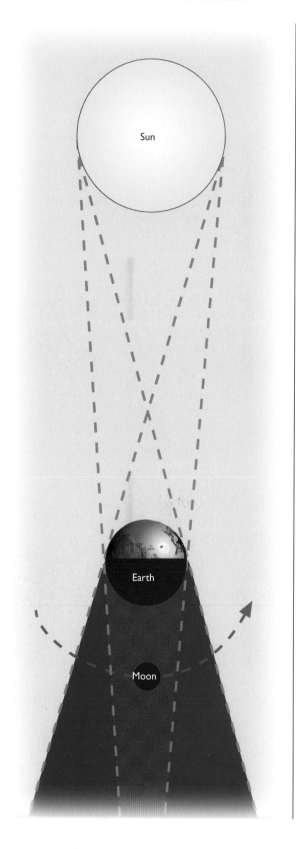

Sun

Earth

Moon

Captured Rotation

From Earth, we always see the same side of the Moon. That is because the Moon rotates once around in space in 27⅓ days, which is exactly the same amount of time it takes to orbit Earth. Several other moons have the same kind of motion, spinning around once in the same amount of time it takes them to orbit their home planet. Astronomers call this a captured rotation. It seems to be a natural rhythm of the universe.

Into the Shadows

The Moon travels in a more or less circular orbit around Earth. And Earth travels in a more or less circular orbit around the Sun. Twice a month, the Sun, Earth, and Moon line up roughly in space—at the time of full moon and new moon.

They only line up roughly because the Sun, the Moon, and Earth do not travel in quite the same plane, or flat sheet, in space.

But just a few times a year, the three bodies line up exactly in space. At times, Earth moves exactly into line between the Sun and the Moon, and its shadow falls on the Moon. We call this an eclipse of the Moon or a lunar eclipse. At other times the

Moon moves exactly into line between the Sun and Earth, and its shadow falls on Earth. This is called an eclipse of the Sun or a solar eclipse.

Eclipse of the Sun

The most spectacular eclipses are eclipses of the Sun. They take place at a new moon. Because the Moon is a small body, it casts a small shadow, which only ever covers a small area of Earth's surface.

If you are in this area during an eclipse, you will first see the Moon edging across the face of the Sun. The light will gradually start to fade. Then, when the Moon covers up the face of the Sun completely, the sky will get dark. Night will fall—during the day. We call this a total eclipse.

But total darkness will last for only a short time—about 7 minutes at most. Then the Moon moves on, the Sun reappears, and day returns once more.

Sometimes the Moon doesn't quite cover up the Sun—we call this a partial eclipse. Sometimes a ring of light remains around the edge of the Moon—we call this an annular (ring) eclipse. On average, two or three solar eclipses of one kind or another take place each year somewhere in the world.

Far left: During an eclipse of the Moon, the Moon moves into the Earth's shadow in space. It can stay in eclipse for more than two hours.

Left: During a lunar eclipse, the Moon does not disappear from view. It turns a pinkish color as it is lit up by light coming from Earth's atmosphere.

Three stages of a solar eclipse:

1. The Moon is gradually covering up the face of the Sun.

2. The Sun's face is now completely covered. The Sun's outer atmosphere, or corona, appears brilliant white.

3. The Moon is just uncovering the edge of the Sun, and the total eclipse is over. This stage is sometimes called the "diamond ring."

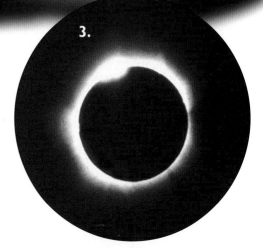

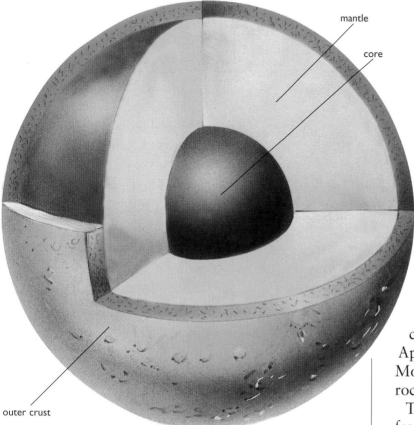

mantle

core

Left: The Moon is made up of several layers. Its hard outer crust is up to about 45 miles (70 km) thick. Then comes a deep layer of rock known as the mantle. At the center is a large core, which may contain metals such as iron.

outer crust

What the Moon is Like

Astronomers sometimes refer to Earth and the Moon as a double planet. They are both rocky bodies that lie close together in space, but in most respects they are very different.

For one thing, their chemical composition is different. The rocks the Apollo astronauts brought back from the Moon are much different, chemically, from rocks on Earth.

The Moon's structure is also different from Earth's. Scientists have worked out the structure by studying "moonquakes," or ground tremors on the Moon. They received information about these from seismometers left behind by the Apollo astronauts.

Below: The Moon has weak gravity and no atmosphere. Astronauts on the Moon have to wear spacesuits in order to breathe.

Weak Gravity

The Moon is much smaller than Earth and therefore has much less mass. This also means that it has a very low gravitational force, or pull. In fact, on the surface it has only one-sixth the gravitational pull of Earth.

The low gravity has largely dictated what the Moon is like. With such low gravity, the Moon also has little atmosphere. Without an atmosphere, there is no weather like we have on Earth—no winds, clouds, rain, or snow. The sky is not blue but black. Without an atmosphere, the Moon is a silent world, because sound needs air to travel through.

Without a "blanket" of air, there is a great difference in temperature on the Moon's surface between day and night. During the day, temperatures rise to more than 100°C—the boiling point of water. During the night, they fall to 150°C below freezing (0°C). A "day" on the moon lasts two weeks on Earth.

Making the Tides

The Moon feels the effect of Earth's gravity. It is Earth's pull that keeps the Moon circling Earth once a month. In its turn, the Moon's gravity—weak though it is—affects Earth. In particular, it causes the tides, the regular rise and fall of the oceans.

When the Moon is overhead, it exerts its strongest gravitational pull on the part of Earth beneath it. Because water is liquid, it is pulled more easily than the land and therefore rises. The result is that water accumulates on the parts of Earth directly beneath and directly opposite the position of the Moon. This is called a high tide, and it

The Moon tugs on the ocean waters beneath it, causing a high tide. It also tugs on Earth and pulls it away from the waters on the opposite side of Earth. In between the high tides, the water falls to create low tides.

occurs twice a day at any given place. The Sun's gravity also affects the tides. The greatest range between high and low tides occur at the new moon, when the Moon and Sun are closest together in the sky, and at the full moon when they are directly opposite.

Moon Data

Diameter at equator: 2160 miles (3476 km)

Mass: 1/81 Earth's mass

Gravity: 1/6 Earth's gravity

Av. distance from Earth: 239,000 miles (384,000 km)

Circles round Earth in: 27½ days

Spins on axis in: 27½ days

Goes through phases in: 29½ days

Birth of the Moon

When the Apollo astronauts returned from the Moon, they brought back many rock samples. Scientists found that the oldest rocks were more than 4 billion years old. The Moon itself must have formed before this, either at the same time as Earth and all the other planets (4.6 billion years ago), or soon after.

No one knows exactly how the Moon was formed. There are several theories. One is that the Moon formed at the same time as Earth. Another is that the Moon was once part of Earth. The newly formed Earth was molten (liquid) and spinning around rapidly. Eventually, it flung off into space a huge blob of molten matter, which cooled and became the Moon.

The trouble with these two ideas is that neither of them explains the differences in chemical make-up and structure between the Moon and Earth. A theory that does explain these differences is that the Moon was formed in another part of the solar system from different materials. Sometime long ago, it strayed near Earth and was captured by Earth's gravitational pull. However, no one has been able to give a good explanation of how this happened.

Impact

The most convincing explanation of how the Moon was formed suggests that it was created as the result of a collision between another large body and the newborn Earth. The force of this body—which could have been as big as Mars—smashing into Earth ripped off a big lump of Earth matter. This matter mixed with matter from the colliding body and became the Moon.

Cooling Down

However the Moon formed, it would first have been in a molten state. Then it slowly cooled, and a wrinkled skin, or crust, formed over it. At this time, space was full of great chunks of rock that had not yet formed into planets or moons. These chunks rained down on the young Moon and dug great craters in its surface hundreds of miles across. This bombardment lasted for hundreds of millions of years.

While the Moon's crust cooled, the rocks inside were heating up. This happened because of radioactivity. Radiation substances in the rocks gave off radiation and also heat. Over time they melted and oozed out as lava into the great pits dug by the chunks of rocks from outer space. The lava spread out to form vast flat plains.

These are the plains referred to today as the moon's "seas." Many are still surrounded by circular mountain ranges that were created as the result of the original collisions.

Most of the craters found on the Moon were created during the fierce bombardment of the surface that happened billions of years ago.

THE LUNAR SURFACE

The Moon's surface has remained more or less as it is today for nearly three billion years. It displays a multitude of fascinating features—vast dusty plains, soaring mountain ranges, and craters galore.

Some features of the Moon's surface can be seen even with the naked eye. Two main regions can be detected—light and dark. The Italian astronomer Galileo first used a telescope to look at the Moon in 1609. He observed that the dark areas were flat regions and the light areas were highlands.

Comparing the Moon's surface with Earth's, he called the flat regions *maria,* or seas, and the highlands *terrae,* or continents. As more powerful telescopes were developed, it became apparent that the flat regions were not watery seas, but dry plains. Even so, the term "seas" is still used to refer to these lunar regions.

There are craters all over the Moon. There are fewer of them, however, on the seas than in the highlands. This tells scientists that the seas are much younger than the highlands. Astronomers think that the highlands are part of the Moon's original crust.

As well as craters, the Moon has many other distinctive features. These include domes, which are swellings of the crust made by lava pushing up. There are long trenches that snake across the surface, sometime for 100 miles (160 km) or more. Called rills, they probably formed when channels or tubes carrying lava collapsed. Most of these features are typical of the lunar seas.

The highest parts of the highlands are the mountain ranges surrounding the seas. They rise as high as 20,000 feet (6,000 meters).

The Apollo astronauts explored both sea and highland regions when they explored the Moon on foot in the 1960s and 1970s. On their six landing missions, they roamed the surface for more than 80 hours and brought back 850 pounds (385 kg) of Moon rocks. They also took thousands of stunning photographs. These expeditions remain the only human exploration of another heavenly body.

The lunar surface has been shaped by rocky bombardment from outer space and also by volcanic processes going on in the Moon's interior. The landscape is barren, with a beauty all its own.

Moonwatch

The picture opposite shows the Moon, as we see it once a month, at the time of the full moon. Some of the main seas, mountains, and craters are marked. If you cover the left-hand side with a sheet of paper, what remains visible is the Moon's eastern hemisphere (half). This is how the Moon appears at its first quarter phase, when it is about 7 days old (7 days after new moon).

The Eastern Half

Several seas are found in the eastern hemisphere (half) of the Moon. Four of them merge into one another—the seas of Serenity, Tranquillity, Fertility, and Nectar. The first Apollo landing took place on the Sea of Tranquillity on July 20, 1969. The easiest sea to spot lies near the eastern limb (edge). It is the small Sea of Crises, which is about 300 miles (500 km) across.

The high ranges of the Apennines and the Caucasus Mountains separate the Sea of Serenity from the Sea of Showers to the west. Peaks in these ranges soar to 20,000 feet (6,000 meters) or more. In the north, a prominent valley, called Alpine Valley, links the Sea of Showers with the Sea of Cold.

Of the craters in this hemisphere, Aristoteles and Eudoxus are prominent in the north. A line of large craters runs south from the center, beginning with the 92-mile (150-km) wide Ptolemaeus. These craters are best seen at the first quarter phase, when they show up on the terminator—the boundary between the lit and unlit parts of the Moon.

The Western Half

If you cover the right-hand side of the picture opposite, you will see the Moon's western hemisphere. This is how you will see the Moon at its last quarter phase, when it is about 21 days old.

This half of the Moon is dominated by two huge seas, the circular Sea of Showers and the sprawling Ocean of Storms. The Sea of Showers is the largest of the circular seas, measuring more than 700 miles (1,100 km) across. It merges into the Ocean of Storms, which extends over an area of over 2,000,000 square miles (5,000,000 sq km), or about two-thirds the size of the United States.

On and around the edge of the Sea of Showers are prominent craters, such as the dark-floored Plato, Archimedes, and Copernicus. Copernicus and nearby Kepler show up brilliantly at full moon, when they are ringed by bright rays. But even they are outshone by Tycho, whose brilliant rays stretch for hundreds of miles.

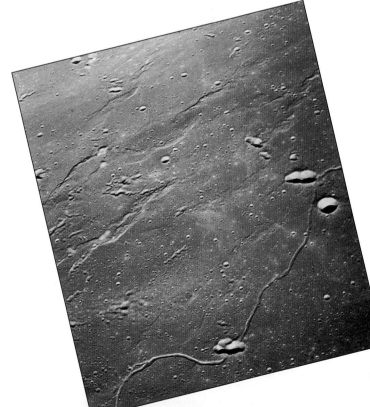

The surface of the Sea of Tranquillity. Like the other seas, it is relatively flat and smooth. Little ridges and channels snake across the surface. They were made by lava flows pushing up under the surface, or flowing over it.

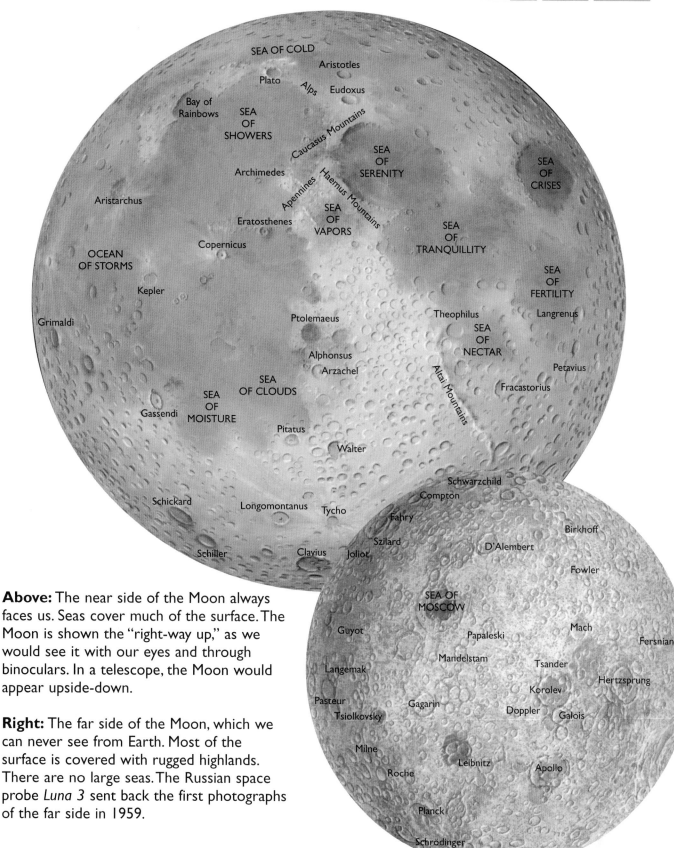

SEA OF COLD
Aristotles
Plato
Alps
Eudoxus
Bay of
Rainbows
SEA
OF
SHOWERS
Caucasus Mountains
SEA
OF
SERENITY
SEA
OF
CRISES
Archimedes
Haemus Mountains
Apennines
SEA
OF
VAPORS
Aristarchus
Eratosthenes
SEA
OF
TRANQUILLITY
Copernicus
OCEAN
OF
STORMS
Kepler
SEA
OF
FERTILITY
Ptolemaeus
Theophilus
Langrenus
Grimaldi
SEA
OF
NECTAR
Alphonsus
Arzachel
Petavius
Altai Mountains
Fracastorius
Gassendi
SEA
OF
MOISTURE
SEA
OF CLOUDS
Pitatus
Walter
Schwarzchild
Compton
Schickard
Longomontanus
Tycho
Fahry
Birkhoff
Szilard
D'Alembert
Schiller
Clavius
Joliot
Fowler
SEA OF
MOSCOW
Guyot
Mach
Papaleski
Fersnian
Mandelstam
Tsander
Langemak
Hertzsprung
Korolev
Pasteur
Gagarin
Doppler
Galois
Tsiolkovsky
Milne
Leibnitz
Apollo
Roche
Planck
Schrödinger

Above: The near side of the Moon always faces us. Seas cover much of the surface. The Moon is shown the "right-way up," as we would see it with our eyes and through binoculars. In a telescope, the Moon would appear upside-down.

Right: The far side of the Moon, which we can never see from Earth. Most of the surface is covered with rugged highlands. There are no large seas. The Russian space probe *Luna 3* sent back the first photographs of the far side in 1959.

Craters

Craters are by far the most common feature of the lunar surface. They are found in the seas and the highland regions. Almost all of the craters were made by meteorites colliding with the Moon. A few are volcanic craters, meaning that they are the openings of volcanoes that erupted long ago.

Craters come in all sizes, from shallow dents in the ground to depressions more than 100 miles (160 km) across. The biggest one that can be easily seen on the Moon's nearside is called Clavius. It measures some 145 miles (260 km) across.

Most large craters have walls higher than the surrounding area and floors that are lower. The floor of a crater called Newton is more than 5.5 miles (9 km) deep. Many large craters also have another feature—a central mountain range.

Craters Old and New

Over time, craters themselves might be hit by meteorites. In the process they can become damaged, or "ruined." Their walls might be knocked down, or new craters are formed within the old one. Sometimes craters become so filled with lava that little of them remains. These are often called ghost craters.

Some of the large newer craters show up brilliantly at full moon because of their rays—lines of shiny material leading from them like the rays of the Sun. The rays consist of material thrown out when the crater was formed.

Right: Craters cover nearly the whole of the far side of the Moon. This heavily cratered region is thought to be part of the Moon's original crust, little changed for billions of years.

Below: A stunning view of the crater Copernicus, taken by an orbiting space probe. Note the step-like terraced walls and the central mountain range, which are typical of the large lunar craters.

Moon Rocks

We know a lot about Moon rocks because of the samples collected by the Apollo astronauts. In general, they are similar to some rocks found on our own planet. They are all igneous ("fire-formed"), which means they formed when molten rock cooled. Many were formed when volcanoes erupted on the Moon billions of years ago.

There are no sedimentary rocks on the Moon as there are on Earth. Sedimentary rocks form from layers of sediment—material that settles out of rivers and seas. Of course, there has never been any great amount of water on the Moon, let alone rivers or seas.

Basalts and Breccias

There are two common kinds of Moon rocks. One is dark-colored and made up of tiny crystals. It is like the rock known as basalt on Earth.

The other main type is a mixture of rock chips cemented together. It was formed when meteorites hit the surface, melting some rocks and shattering others. The molten rock flowed over bits of broken rock and cemented them together. This type of rock is called breccia.

Above: Human beings from planet Earth left their footprints in the lunar soil, which is known as *regolith*. The soil is a mixture of fine dust, rock chips, and minute glass beads.

Above: A common type of Moon rock called breccia, made up of rock chips cemented together.

Left: A typical light-colored Moon rock, like some volcanic rocks we find on Earth.

Project Apollo

To send astronauts to the Moon and bring them back safely to Earth required an extraordinary effort on the part of thousands of people who worked with the U.S. government organization known as NASA (National Aeronautics and Space Administration). For the Apollo project, which was the name given to the Moon-landing effort, a new generation of spacecraft and rockets had to be developed. Astronauts had to be trained in the techniques needed to bring about a lunar landing and a safe return. This took time and money—about $25 billion by the time the project had finished.

Lunar Orbit Rendezvous

The method NASA developed to land astronauts on the Moon was called lunar orbit rendezvous. It centered on the three-man Apollo spacecraft. The whole spacecraft would set out for the Moon. Then, in lunar orbit, a landing vehicle would separate from the main "mother ship" and descend to the lunar surface. Later, it would take off from the surface and rendezvous (meet) with the mother ship,

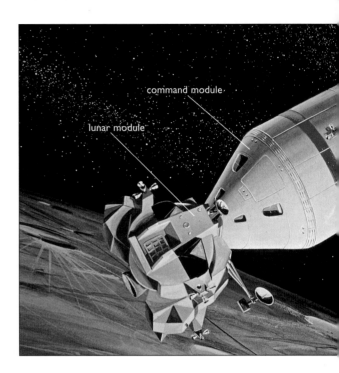

which would then return to Earth.

The Apollo spacecraft was made up of three modules (parts). The crew occupied the command module, which was pressurized with oxygen for the crew to breathe. This was joined for most of the time with an equipment, or service, module, which had a powerful rocket engine. The command and service modules together formed the CSM mother ship.

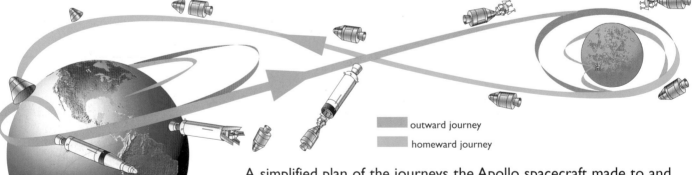

outward journey

homeward journey

A simplified plan of the journeys the Apollo spacecraft made to and from the Moon. They were launched by *Saturn V* from Florida, then separated and flew to the Moon. The lunar module dropped down to the surface, then carried its two astronauts back to the mother ship, which returned to Earth. Just before re-entering the atmosphere, the command module separated and splashed down in the Pacific Ocean.

service module

Left: The three-man Apollo spacecraft, shown as it neared the Moon, with the lunar module still linked with the command module.

Right: A *Saturn V* rocket waits for blast off at the launch pad, with the command module on top. This is the only part of this mammoth launch vehicle that will return to Earth.

For the trip to the Moon, the CSM was linked to the landing vehicle, the lunar module (LM). This was built to take two of the astronauts down to the surface. They lifted off the Moon in the upper part of the LM, using the lower part as a launch pad.

Mighty Moon Rocket

Rocket pioneer Wernher von Braun was the mastermind behind the powerful rocket needed to launch the 45-ton Apollo spacecraft to the Moon. This rocket, the *Saturn V,* was gigantic. With the Apollo spacecraft on top, it stood 365 feet (111 meters) tall and weighed nearly 3,000 tons.

To launch the *Saturn V,* a new launch site was built just inland from Cape Canaveral in Florida. It was named the Kennedy Space Center after John F. Kennedy, the president who launched the Apollo Project. The site featured two launch pads and a huge Vehicle Assembly Building (VAB), where the Moon rockets were put together. Today, the Kennedy Space Center is the focus for space shuttle operations.

Men on the Moon

A *Saturn V* first carried astronauts to the Moon in December 1968. It was a test mission *(Apollo 8)*, which orbited the Moon on Christmas Eve and returned without landing. Television viewers back on planet Earth were able to see the surface of the Moon in close-up for the first time. What a sight it was!

The following July, *Apollo 11* set off to attempt the first Moon landing. On July 20, 1969, the *Apollo 11* lunar module (code-named *Eagle*) touched down on the Sea of Tranquillity. Reported lunar module commander Neil Armstrong to mission control at Houston: "Tranquillity Base here. The *Eagle* has landed."

A few hours later Armstrong became the first man to set foot on the Moon. "That's one small step for man," he said, "one giant leap for mankind." And so it was. A being from planet Earth had set foot on another world.

Opposite, main picture: The most famous Apollo picture, showing Edwin Aldrin on the Sea of Tranquillity during the *Apollo 11* mission in July 1969. **Inset:** The *Apollo 11* crew, from the left: Neil Armstrong, Michael Collins, and Edwin "Buzz" Aldrin.

Right, main picture: On the last three Apollo missions the astronauts were able to wander farther afield because they had transportation—the lunar rover, or Moon buggy. **Inset:** All the Apollo missions splashed down in the Pacific Ocean, lowered gently into the sea by three huge parachutes.

Moonwalking

Armstrong was the first of 12 astronauts to leave footprints in the lunar soil. Over the next three-and-a-half years, they explored the lunar seas and highlands, first on foot and then with the help of a lunar rover, nicknamed the "Moon buggy."

The astronauts had a punishing workload, planned in detail beforehand. They picked up rocks and also drilled into the ground for samples. They also set up scientific stations, using a package of different instruments called ALSEP (Apollo lunar surface experiments package).

A nuclear battery powered the equipment, which included a seismometer to detect tremors in the ground, or "moonquakes." The ALSEP scientific stations radioed the data they collected back to scientists on Earth and continued to do so until 1977.

"We Shall Return"

Apollo 17 commander Eugene Cernan took the last step on the Moon on December 14, 1972. Just before he left, he made this promise: "We leave as we came and, God willing, we shall return with peace and hope for all mankind."

No doubt human beings will one day return to the Moon. This time they will probably build permanent residences and set up scientific bases, observatories, and mining camps as well. The recent discovery of water (as ice) in some lunar craters means that future bases could be more self-supporting.

Glossary

ASTEROIDS Small lumps of rock or metal that circle the Sun. Most circle in a broad band (the asteroid belt) between the orbits of Mars and Jupiter.

ATMOSPHERE The layer of gases around a planet or another heavenly body.

CHROMOSPHERE The inner part of the Sun's atmosphere.

CLIMATE The average kind of weather a place experiences during the year.

CORE The center part of a body.

CORONA The outer part of the Sun's atmosphere.

CRATER A circular pit in the surface of a planet or moon, caused by a ite or asteroid.

CRUST The hard outer layer of a planet or a moon.

ECLIPSE What happens when one body in space covers up another, such an eclipse of the Sun, when the Moon covers up the Sun.

ELECTROMAGNETIC WAVES Waves and rays given out by the Sun.

FALLING STAR A popular name for a meteor.

FLARE A massive explosion on the Sun.

GALAXY A "star island" in space. Our own galaxy is called the Milky Way.

GRAVITY The pull, or force of attraction, that every body has because of its mass.

LUNAR To do with the Moon.

METEOR A streak of light produced when a meteoroid burns up in Earth's atmosphere.

METEORITE A piece of rock or metal that falls to the ground from outer space.

MOON The common name for a satellite.

MOONQUAKE A ground vibration, or tremor, on the Moon.

NEBULA A cloud of gas and dust in space.

NUCLEAR REACTION A process that involves the nuclei (centers) of atoms.

NUCLEUS The center of an atom.

ORBIT The path in space one body follows when it circles around another, such as the Moon's orbit around Earth.

PHASES The changes in appearance of the Moon in the night sky as the month goes by.

PHOTOSPHERE The glaring surface of the Sun.

PLANET One of nine bodies that circle around the Sun; or more generally, a large body that circles around a star.

PROBE A spacecraft sent to explore other heavenly bodies, such as planets, moons, asteroids, and comets.

PROMINENCE A great fountain of hot gas that shoots out from the Sun.

SATELLITE A small body that orbits around a larger one; a moon. Also the usual name for an artificial satellite, an orbiting spacecraft.

SEA A large, flat plain on the Moon, which astronomers call *mare* (plural, *maria*).

SEASONS Periods of the year when there are noticeable differences in the temperature and weather.

SHOOTING STAR A popular name for a meteor.

SOLAR To do with the Sun.

SOLAR SYSTEM The Sun and the bodies that circle around it, including planets, comets, and asteroids.

SOLAR WIND A stream of charged particles given off by the Sun.

STAR A huge ball of very hot gas, which gives off energy as light, heat, and other radiation.

STELLAR To do with the stars.

SUNSPOT A darker, cooler region of the Sun's surface.

TIDES The regular falling and rising of ocean waters, caused mainly by the Moon's gravity.

UNIVERSE Space and everything that is in it—galaxies, stars, planets, moons, and energy.

Important Dates

1543 Nicolaus Copernicus suggests a solar system

1609 Galileo looks at the Moon for the first time with a telescope

1610 Galileo discovers sunspots

1733 The Swedish astronomer Vasenius studies prominences during a solar eclipse

1801 J. Ritter discovers that the Sun gives out ultraviolet radiation

1802 W. H. Wollaston discovers dark lines in the Sun's spectrum, from which astronomers eventually determined the Sun's make-up

1840 J. W. Draper takes the first photographs of the Moon

1851 H. Schwabe discovers the regular sunspot cycle of 11 years

1908 George Hale first measures the Sun's magnetism

1959 The *Luna 2* probe crash-lands on the Moon

1966 *Surveyor 1* makes a soft landing on the Moon and transmits the first close-up photographs of its surface

1968 *Apollo 8* carries the first astronauts to the Moon and back, but doesn't land

1969 *Apollo 11* makes the first Moon landing

1972 The final Apollo mission *(Apollo 17)* takes place

1973 Astronauts on the U.S. space station *Skylab* make a detailed study of the Sun

1991 One of the longest solar eclipses of the century is observed from Hawaii

1995 The *SOHO* probe is launched to study the Sun

1998 The *Lunar Prospector* probe discovers ice in lunar craters

Further Reading

Large numbers of books on astronomy and space are available in school and public libraries. Librarians will be happy to help you find them. In addition, publishers display their books on the Internet, and you can key into their websites and search for astronomy books. Alternatively, you can look at the websites of on-line bookshops (such as Amazon.com) and search for books on astronomy and space. Here are just a selection of recently published books for further reading.

Backyard Astronomy by Robert Burnham, Time-Life, 2001

Comet Science by Jacques Crovisier and Therese Encrenaz, Cambridge, 1999

Exploring the Night Sky with Binoculars by Patrick Moore, Cambridge, 2000

Field Guide to Stars and Planets by Jay Pasachoff, Houghton Mifflin, 1999

Get a Grip on Astronomy by Robin Kerrod, Time-Life, 1999

Introduction to Astronomy by Nick Shaffer, Random House, 1999

Night Sky by Gary Mechler, National Audubon Society, 1999

Observing the Moon by Peter Wlasuk, Springer, 1999

Target Earth by Duncan Steel, Time-Life, 2000

The Young Astronomer by Sheila Snowden, EDC Publications, 2000

Websites

Astronomy and space are popular topics on the Internet, and there are hundreds of interesting websites—details about the latest eclipse, mission to Mars and SETI (Search for Extraterrestrial Intelligence), and so forth.

A good place to start is by using a Search Engine, and search for space and astronomy. Search engines will display extensive listings of topics, which you can then select. For example, you gain access to a list of topics on the Search Engine Yahoo on astronomy with: **http://yahoo.com/Science/Astronomy**

The lists also includes astronomy clubs. If there is one near you, you may well like to join it. Most clubs have interesting programs, with observing evenings, lectures, and visits to observatories.

NASA has many websites covering all aspects of space science, including exploration of the planets and the universe as a whole. The best place to start is at NASA's home page: **http://www.nasa.gov**

From there you can go to, for example, Space Science, which includes planetary exploration. Or you can go directly to: **http://spacescience.nasa.gov/missions**

Individual missions may also have their own website, such as the Mars Odyssey mission at: **http:/mars.jpl.nasa.gov/Odyssey**

The latest information and images from the Hubble Space Telescope can be reached at: **http:/www.stsci.edu/pubinfo** This site will also direct you to picture highlights since the launch of the Telescope in 1990.

European space science activities can be explored via the home page of the European Space Agency at: **http:/www.esa.int**

Index